The Wild and the Sacred

VOLUME 1

The Wild and the Sacred

*Evaluating and Protecting
the Ocmulgee River Corridor*

CHRIS WATSON
EDITED BY S. HEATHER DUNCAN

MERCER UNIVERSITY OCMULGEE SERIES
VOLUME 1

MERCER UNIVERSITY PRESS
MACON, GEORGIA

MUP/ P653

© 2022 by Mercer University Press
Published by Mercer University Press
1501 Mercer University Drive
Macon, Georgia 31207
All rights reserved

26 25 24 23 22   5 4 3 2 1

Books published by Mercer University Press are printed on
acid-free paper that meets the requirements of the American
National Standard for Information Sciences—Permanence
of Paper for Printed Library Materials.

Printed and bound in the United States.

Text is set in Meta Pro Serif, 10.5/13;
display is set in Clarendon Text pro;
captions are set in Meta Pro, 8/9

Book design by Burt&Burt.

ISBN 978-0-88146-863-2

Cataloging-in-Publication Data is available
from the Library of Congress

Table of Contents

Acknowledgments

Dedicated to the people of the Muscogee (Creek) Nation and to the people of Macon and Middle Georgia. May this work, in some small way, contribute to the rejoining of what has been separated—both the land and its creatures as well as the peoples.

Many thanks to the photographers who donated their labor and artistry to this book: Sharman Ayoub, Alan Cressler, Sylvia Flowers, Jim Gilreath, Doug Kimball, Christopher I. Smith, John Wilson, and Bobby Bond and Scott McDonald with the Georgia Department of Natural Resources.

The Wild and the Sacred

VOLUME 1

CHAPTER 1

In Search of Wildness

The Ocmulgee River winds through the middle of Georgia, unspooling wildness. On its banks, black bears lumber through forests where bald eagles nest. Fleeting flowers bloom on chalk prairies that swim with the fossilized bones of whales. For a region only an hour south of Atlanta, it's remarkably undeveloped.

In 2008, a University of Georgia study evaluated this Ocmulgee River corridor for both its natural and cultural value. The area, stretching from Macon south to Hawkinsville, is home to some of the wildest unprotected land in Georgia. These findings justified a much greater focus on its conservation by the state, nonprofits, and the federal government, potentially including the National Park Service.

The Ocmulgee River. *Photo by Sharman Ayoub*

Photo by Christopher Smith

Researcher Chris Watson began by developing a tool for mapping wildness across the Georgia landscape. But as work progressed, the study's conception of the region's significance expanded beyond ecology: the floodplain's value is immeasurable to the Muscogee Indians. As the earliest people to settle the Southeast, their ancestors left a physical imprint on the land, from the remains of villages to giant earthen mounds. In turn, the land left a spiritual imprint upon the Muscogee that is still felt today. As a result, interest converges in protecting the wild and the sacred.

The results of Watson's study boosted local efforts to create a large new national park unit or something similar, perhaps through expanding upon the existing Ocmulgee Mounds National Historical Park in Macon.

The UGA study had four major objectives:

1. Measure the degree of wildness in the Georgia landscape.
2. Contrast mapping approaches that focus on wildness with those that focus on biodiversity.
3. Summarize arguments for expanding an Ocmulgee Mounds park and linking it to other existing protected lands along the Ocmulgee River. (At the time of the initial study, the park was

Ocmulgee Mounds National Historical Park. *Photo by Christopher Smith.*

called Ocmulgee National Monument; it's now a national historical park).

4. Survey contemporary Muscogee people in Oklahoma about their values and attitudes regarding the tribe's historic homeland in Georgia.

Setting the Stage

The Ocmulgee River flows from its source south of Atlanta to feed the Altamaha River at Lumber City. This study primarily focuses on the conservation value of the lands surrounding the eighty-three river miles between Macon and Hawkinsville.

In Macon, the river passes the Ocmulgee Mounds National Historical Park. Here, prehistoric Native Americans built ceremonial mounds that were excavated during the Great Depression. In 1936, roughly 678 acres were designated as a national monument.

In March of 2019, the US Congress approved renaming the park and quadrupling its size to roughly 2,800 acres. However, for additional acres to be added, property must be donated or bought from willing sellers. The park and its nonprofit and community partners are in the process of accepting some land donations. Almost 20 percent of the land within the extended boundary has already been donated by the Macon Housing Authority or Macon/Bibb County and transferred to the park in the first half of 2020.

When it enlarged the park, Congress also gave the US Department of the Interior three years to conduct a "Special Resource Study" that would evaluate the significance of its resources, then make recommendations about whether the park should be even larger—and if so, how it should change and who should manage it. For decades, groups of local citizens have rallied support for the river corridor's potential to host a big game preserve or a national park, options which could offer better protection than the current patchwork of distant managers and owners.

In the stretch between Macon and Hawkinsville, the Ocmulgee River is mostly a dark, slow wanderer. It often remains out of sight until crossed by the occasional country bridge.

(Left) Middle Georgia black bear cubs. *Photo by Bobby Bond, courtesy the Georgia Wildlife Resources Division.* (Right) Gray fox. *Photo by Sharman Ayoub.*

But animals move within, over, and around it. This is partly because of public land south of Ocmulgee Mounds. Here, the US Fish and Wildlife Service manages Bond Swamp National Wildlife Refuge and Brown's Mount, and the state operates a series of wildlife management areas. Two of these are home base for Middle Georgia's black bear population.

The river also has a magnetic pull for migratory songbirds, Mississippi shrikes, and many more species. The undeveloped-stream terraces and uplands near its shores are home to endangered or rare plants such as fringed campion, Ocmulgee skullcap, and Durand oak.

Development pressure has already threatened key natural lands such as Oaky Woods Wildlife Management Area, one of the most popular public hunting areas in the state. Nearby, Warner Robins has seen rapid population growth around the region's largest employer, Robins Air Force Base. At the same time, Atlanta's sprawl pushes south toward Macon, a city of about 150,000 people.

The Georgia Wildlands Assessment

The Wilderness Society, a national nonprofit, recognized these pressures more than a decade ago. Unlike in the American West, much less of the wild land in the South is publicly owned. In the late 1990s, a small group within the Wilderness Society concluded that the conservation landscape had changed so much—literally and figuratively—that its focus on federal public land was too limited.

The organization envisioned partnerships to build a "Network of Wild Lands" through collaboration with private landowners, providing tools such as economic assessments and mapping. The network could then include not only public land but also private forests as well as regional natural areas like greenways.

But first, the Wilderness Society needed to set priorities for this broadened mission: Which parts of populous states remained the wildest? And just what would "wildness" mean in a region that had been cleared and settled for centuries?

The Wilderness Society asked the University of Georgia Center for Remote Sensing and Mapping Science (now called the Center for Geospatial Research) for help creating a wilderness-mapping

(Left) Beaver lodge. *Photo by Sharman Ayoub.* (Above Right) A limpkin at Ocmulgee Public Fishing Area. *Photo by Barbara Edwards.* (Below right) White-tail deer fawn. *Photo by Sharman Ayoub.*

tool. The project was originally envisioned as a prototype that could be used across the South and perhaps elsewhere in the United States. Georgia was chosen for the prototype because the state was urbanizing so quickly. The resulting study came to be known as the "Georgia Wildlands Assessment."

However, the Wilderness Society switched gears and discontinued its Network of Wild Lands initiative before the study was finished. Over the years, the concept of partnering with private landowners and linking conservation lands has evolved and spread, especially through the growing land trust movement. The UGA study generated both a wildness map and concrete recommendations for governments and conservation organizations. The map showed an area of high potential in the Ocmulgee River corridor—the wildest region in the state at that time that hadn't been widely recognized, studied, or protected as such.

Stronger conservation measures are clearly needed for the region. But what properties should be conserved, and what steps should be taken? These are some of the questions this study tackled.

CHAPTER 2

An Old Dream Renewed

The Case for Protecting the River Corridor

Although the National Park Service has only recently begun studying whether land along the Ocmulgee River deserves more protection, the idea is far from new.

In the waning days of World War II, a group called the Ocmulgee Valley Association promoted creating a 200,000-acre big game preserve along the river between Macon and Hawkinsville. If that had happened, then Macon would now have an asset on its doorstep comparable to Great Smoky Mountains National Park. (In 2019, America's most popular national park welcomed more than 12.5 million visitors. The year before, 11.4 million visitors contributed $953 million to the local economy.)

In more recent times, Macon environmental activist John Wilson proposed expanding the Ocmulgee National Monument into a national park at least as far back as 1992. Despite his influence in establishing Bond Swamp as a national wildlife refuge in 1989, Wilson's national park idea was widely regarded as a pipe dream.

Photo by Sharman Ayoub

Left, John Wilson loads up bald eagle decoys during his campaign to protect Bond Swamp, where eagles nest, in the 1980s. *Photo courtesy John Wilson.* Right, Boaters in Bond Swamp. *Photo by John Wilson.*

That began to change as the threat of development became more concrete. In 2004, a group of Houston County developers bought close to 20,000 acres along the Ocmulgee River in Houston County. The previous owner, Weyerhaeuser timber company, had long leased the land to the state for public hunting as Oaky Woods Wildlife Management Area. Although it is home to rare ecosystems and black bears, the sale left it slated for a 30,000-home development.

This threat helped galvanize the creation of a citizen stakeholder group called the Central Georgia Rivers Partnership. Hunting advocates, state and federal public land managers, conservation nonprofits, and other interested locals met to share their ideas and research. While they didn't agree on a unified plan, it marked the beginning of greater collaboration for conserving land around the river.

The partnership stopped meeting after about a year and a half, although its members and the public continued the push to protect Oaky Woods. Development plans there were stalled by the 2008 recession. In 2011, public outcry led the state to buy about 10,000 acres.

Meanwhile, Wilson's "big park" idea gained traction. To the Central Georgia Rivers Partnership, he initially suggested three alternatives for the park's size. These ranged from 48,000 acres to 82,000 acres. The goal was to link about 27,000 acres of existing publicly owned or managed lands along the Ocmulgee River. Fifteen years later, Wilson says that continuous link from Macon to Hawkinsville remains feasible.

An Economic Boost

Wilson voiced a number of pocketbook arguments for a national park. First, fragmented ownership—even fragmented *public* ownership, divided among state and federal departments—is less efficient. It doesn't achieve economies of scale in protecting and managing resources. For example, local refuges, parks, and wildlife management areas don't often coordinate on operations such as controlled burns, law enforcement, or visitor services.

This lack of coordination also prevents effective marketing of public lands, along with their recreation opportunities, to potential visitors. Many of these public lands don't even appear on road maps. When their considerable tourism potential isn't realized, nearby communities lose out.

National parks are considered the jewels of the park system and often attract significantly more visitors than other kinds of parks. Having Atlanta and its international airport so nearby would make the Ocmulgee easy to reach and easy to market outside the region.

A national park could provide a stable employer and economic driver, even as the region's skilled manufacturing industries drain away. (Unlike a private company, a national park can't relocate to another state or country.)

Visitors gaze over the wetland from the top of the Great Temple Mound in Ocmulgee Mounds National Historical Park. *Photo by Christopher Smith.*

BENEFITS TO ROBINS AIR FORCE BASE

A national park and preserve bordering Robins Air Force Base could help protect the viability of the base, which borders a large swath of undeveloped land between Macon and Hawkinsville.

Fast, uncontrolled development near US military installations has begun to erode military training and preparation nationwide. Robins is no exception.

Housing fifty-four mission partners and employing 23,000 people, Robins must compete with other military bases to survive periodic "Base Realignment and Closure" evaluations. Development pressure near a base is a strike against it. Public exposure to military chemicals, noise, dust, and weapons testing is a safety hazard. Plus, businesses and residents may begin to demand limits on base activities that could pose a risk to a growing population of nearby neighbors. This can come into conflict with the US Department of Defense's need for bases that can adapt their missions to evolving world events and new technology.

Robins has already purchased property from residents to its north to create a buffer zone for jet-flight paths. Many states are trying to help protect military bases from conflicts with neighbors. Georgia, for example, requires local communities to seek the base commander's recommendations before approving nearby zoning changes or developments.

At the beginning of 2020, Robins planned to start a new joint land-use study to examine how military needs fit with surrounding land uses. It's a good opportunity for the base to consider whether it needs further buffer zones. Preserving surrounding land would prevent encroachment from development on three sides.

Watson notes an additional benefit of extending a buffer between the base and the Ocmulgee River to the east: Robins could more fully participate in the Sentinel Landscape Partnership. Only certain military installations, including Robins, are eligible for this collaboration between the defense, agriculture, and interior departments. The program aims to protect working lands, preserve wildlife habitat, and sustain military readiness by focusing on places where these priorities overlap.

Sentinel Landscape partners work to preserve the ecosystems and rural character of surrounding land so wildlife has a home outside military property. (Otherwise, encroaching development can both compromise military training and make the base an inadvertent refuge for threatened species—possibly further limiting its operations.) Active participation in the Sentinel program could weigh in favor of the base during realignment and closure evaluations.

Inside of a hanger at Robins Air Force Base. *Photo courtesy U.S. Air Force.*

Left, boating on the Ocmulgee. *Photo by Sharman Ayoub.* Right, the Ocmulgee River Corridor is a popular spot for birders seeking to spot migratory song birds, birds of prey and water fowl. *Photo by Jim Gilreath.*

One difficulty with Wilson's concept, however, was that it didn't guarantee the protection of public hunting, an important recreational activity in Middle Georgia. A solution to this challenge was found in the dual concept of a national park and preserve, in which the preserve component would permanently protect public hunting rights. This will be further discussed later in this chapter.

In 2017, a study by the National Parks Conservation Association using economists at the University of Tennessee found that an Ocmulgee National Park and Preserve would likely generate more than $206 million in annual economic activity, 90 percent of which would come from increases in visitor spending. Researchers predicted a national park would attract six times as many visitors over fifteen years, leading to the opening of new businesses such as campgrounds, sporting-goods outfitters, tour guides, restaurants, and hotels.

The concept picked up steam among local business and political leaders. Even before the University of Tennessee economic study was completed, resolutions of support for expanding the park boundary were passed by seven cities, four county development authorities, and two chambers of commerce. The Park Service received more than 3,230 supportive comments during a public-comment period in 2014. Only one commenter opposed it (and he changed his mind).

Paths to a Larger Park

There are two main paths for expanding or significantly changing a property managed by the National Park Service. The first is an administrative decision to make a minor boundary adjustment to a current park. The second would require Congress to designate a new park unit. (In some ways, this is like starting over with a bigger size and mission.)

In addition, a third, less common option is for Congress to establish an umbrella designation for public land that is managed through several agencies working together. The Santa Monica Mountains National Recreation Area is an example within the National Park System.

The Park Service made an administrative decision in 2012 to conduct a boundary study of Ocmulgee, focused on the traditional Ocmulgee Old Fields area associated with the Muscogee (Creek) people and the mounds. Congress considered this study and public feedback before deciding in 2019 to increase the park's size and change its name.

The same legislation authorized another, much broader study, asking the Park Service to gather information about the natural and cultural resources along the river between Macon and Hawkinsville. Unlike the previous boundary study—which focused on cultural and archaeological resources related to prehistoric people and their descendants—this new study will also cover natural and wildlife resources as well as other types of historical resources.

The Park Service has until spring of 2023 to file its report with Congress about whether these resources are so important to the nation that further conservation and management is needed. If so, suggestions will be provided about which agency or mix of agencies should take the action recommended. Depending on the study results and public feedback, a national park and preserve could end up as one proposed option.

There are many types of park "units" in the federal system. They reflect different resources, sizes, and management approaches. At the top tier, national parks are usually very large and protect many resources of national importance.

But this isn't always true. For example, Congaree National Park in South Carolina, another former national monument, was designated in 2003. At 26,000 acres, it's roughly half the minimum size envisioned for Ocmulgee, and it protects only a single nationally significant resource (bottomland hardwood forest).

Before any new unit of the national park system could be created, the Special Resource Study would have to show that it:

Visitors walk to the reconstructed Earth Lodge at Ocmulgee Mounds National Historical Park.

Paddling through Congaree. *Photo courtesy Michelle/HeadAlongwithHeart.com.*

1. would showcase and protect resources that aren't already well represented or well protected for the public at another park;
2. won't be too expensive to create (through buying land) or care for;
3. is both accessible enough and big enough to handle visitors *without* compromising its important features;
4. could be better managed by the Park Service than by anyone else.

But none of this matters if the area doesn't have resources with "national significance." What does that mean? Basically, these would be outstanding and unspoiled examples of each kind of resource, with "superlative opportunities for public enjoyment or for scientific study." These features—whether historical or ecological—must also do an exceptional job of illustrating the themes of our nation's heritage. There are specific criteria for both natural and cultural resources.

Some have suggested that distinctions would have to be drawn between Ocmulgee Mounds and Congaree National Park to justify further elevating the Georgia park. Both feature a rare bottomland hardwood ecosystem. Congaree has more undisturbed old-growth forest.

Left, Butterfly. *Photo by Sharman Ayoub.* Right, the chalk prairies of Oaky Woods are the only ones that support this particular grassland ecosystem. They survived decades of timber company ownership mostly because pines wouldn't grow there. Photo by Alan Cressler, courtesy Southeastern Grasslands Initiative.

CRITERIA FOR EVALUATING RESOURCES

To evaluate whether a proposed addition to the national park system contains nationally significant resources, the Park Service uses a list of ideal principles or illustrations.

For natural areas, these include sites that:
- illustrate the characteristics of a widespread landform or ecosystem;
- contain a rare remnant natural landscape or ecosystem of a type that was once widespread, but is now vanishing due to human settlement and development;
- contain a landform or biotic area that has always been extremely uncommon in the region or nation;
- have exceptional diversity of species, habitats, or ecological communities, or diverse geological features;
- are home to a species or ecosystem unusual for that location;
- harbor a concentrated population of a rare, threatened, or endangered plant or animal;

Eastern Kingbird.
Photo by Doug Kimball.

- provide a critical refuge for the continued survival of a species;
- contain rare or unusually abundant fossil deposits;
- have outstanding scenery;
- are important for a long-term record of research and scientific discovery.

For cultural areas, these include sites that:
- are associated with events that contribute to the broad national patterns of US history and can provide a broad understanding of those patterns;
- are associated with the lives of persons nationally significant in United States history;
- embody features that distinguish an architectural type that illustrates a period, style, or construction method;
- have components that may be worthy individually, but that together illustrate a way of life or culture, or demonstrate historical and artistic significance;
- have produced (or are likely to produce) major scientific discoveries by revealing new cultures or new information about broad periods of human occupation across a region.

However, Congaree lacks the important Native American cultural heritage and archaeological resources that Ocmulgee has. And even from an ecological standpoint, Ocmulgee differs from Congaree in featuring land types besides swamp, such as the Georgia Eocene chalk prairies.

These prairies were once categorized as the easternmost of the "black belt prairies," which occur as far west as Texas. But here the plant community is so different that the Oaky Woods prairies have been identified as a separate type, found nowhere else. These twelve prairies, which range in size from two to twenty acres, are the remains of an ocean floor formed more than sixty-five million years ago. Many marine fossils, including ancient whale skeletons, have been found in the chalk. The prairies could contribute toward a case for "an exceptional diversity of ecological components" worthy of a national park.

Land Use

Watson acknowledges that competing visions about future land use present a possible obstacle to preserving more land in the Ocmulgee corridor. Some local residents and businesses are concerned about loss of traditional hunting grounds or roadblocks to industry.

Some of the staunchest conservationists in Georgia are hunters, and Oaky Woods and Ocmulgee wildlife management areas are among some of the state's most popular public hunting areas. They are also in the heart of the Ocmulgee corridor's black bear habitat. Hunting advocates, such as the Georgia Wildlife Federation, have insisted that any park designation should not limit hunting and fishing in wildlife-management areas and Bond Swamp.

While most national parks don't allow hunting, it's permitted in some other kinds of federal park units, such as national preserves. Ultimately, it's up to Congress to choose what kind of protections the land would receive and spell out what activities can happen there.

Watson's UGA study proposed a solution that has since been embraced by many: designating the area as a "national park and preserve." In this type of designation, the "preserve" portions are designed to support hunting and fishing. The precedent for dual

Left, A hunter poses with a deer he killed at Oaky Woods. *Photo courtesy Georgia Department of Natural Resources.* Right, white-tail doe on alert at dawn. *Photo by Sharman Ayoub.*

designations was established in Alaska to protect subsistence hunting, followed by "park and preserve" units in Colorado and Idaho (both replacing older, smaller national monuments).

At Ocmulgee, stricter national park protections could be limited to the current Ocmulgee Mounds park in addition to the archaeological and cultural sites associated with it.

This would be a "best of both worlds" scenario: the new park unit would receive the increased acclaim attached to a "National Park" while also permanently protecting traditional hunting and fishing areas.

In fact, adding more land could expand public hunting and fishing opportunities even further. Otherwise, many current hunting areas are likely to be lost through privatization, development, and decreasing wildlife populations.

For example, although the state of Georgia bought part of Oaky Woods in 2011, the purchase included only about half the area that had been part of the wildlife management area for decades.

Photo by Sharman Ayoub

CHAPTER 3

Mapping Wildness

A Georgia Case Study

The United States is a world leader in population growth and urbanization, and Georgia is among the states whose farm and forestland is disappearing fastest. A US Forest Service report at the turn of the century estimated that urban sprawl would replace thirty-one million acres of forest in the Southeast by 2040—equal to forty-one Chattahoochee National Forests. To accommodate the booming population, the state adds about a thousand miles of new roads a year, further fragmenting wildlife habitat.

Given these changes, very few places in Georgia can still be considered "wilderness." This is especially true when using the definition established by the US Wilderness Act of 1964. That law

Landscape wildness for the lower 48 states: Blue=high wildness, red=low wildness. *Courtesy of The Wilderness Society.*

Spring in the wetlands near the Ocmulgee Mounds. *Photo by Sharman Ayoub.*

describes wilderness as having a primeval character, "where man himself is a visitor." Under the act, a wilderness area must include at least 5,000 acres—or at least be large enough to function as a place of natural solitude.

All of Georgia's federally designated wilderness areas cluster along the coast and its northern and southern borders. And almost all of it is owned by the federal government. In contrast, most of Middle Georgia's wild lands are privately owned. Exceptions include Bond Swamp National Wildlife Refuge and Robins Air Force Base.

So, how do we identify additional areas there that could still be meaningfully protected for their wildness?

Wildness and Biodiversity

One way to measure wildness is by examining plant and animal populations: wild places might be home to many diverse life forms.

This approach assumes that the concepts of wildness and biodiversity are more or less the same. But they're not. They are distinct approaches to conservation.

A biodiversity-based conservation approach requires listing the array of living things in an area. Then, plans are developed for maintaining that rich variety in the landscape.

A related, but slightly different, approach would preserve at least one species to fill each role in an ecosystem. If several species fill a niche—a large carnivore, say, or a key pollinator—then some species could disappear, as long as at least one continues to serve that purpose.

Both of these strategies encourage people to create the right conditions for specific species to survive.

In contrast, a wilderness approach emphasizes not interfering. The goal is to reduce human impact as much as possible. This doesn't necessarily produce a more diverse plant and animal community.

For example, sometimes only human management keeps conditions right for an endangered species. In Georgia, controlled burning can maintain a longleaf pine ecosystem for endangered red-cockaded woodpeckers; otherwise, the forest might evolve into hardwoods the birds can't use.

However, the wildness approach respects the land's ability to function and adapt on its own. Based on the definition in the Wilderness Act, wilderness isn't just a place where people aren't allowed to build houses and roads (damaging habitat)—it's also a place where people aren't allowed to manipulate the conditions, even to improve habitat. However, even in places that fall short of the strict legislative definition of wilderness, a similar preservation approach might be applied in areas with a high degree of wild character.

The wildness and biodiversity approaches are not necessarily mutually exclusive. But there are practical limits to how much they can be mingled. Given limited resources, conservationists may face the unpleasant dilemma of having to choose between focusing on areas with high wildness but less diversity, or vice versa.

Diversity at the Ocmulgee Mounds. *Photos by Sharman Ayoub.*

PROS AND CONS OF THE WILDNESS APPROACH

UGA focused on a wildness approach when developing its mapping model. Because this is less common than concentrating on species richness, it provides a new tool. It also has the potential to illuminate areas in the Georgia landscape that could be valuable for conservation, even though they don't stand out in existing models focused on biodiversity.

Yet there are some notable philosophical criticisms of the wildness approach. Given how long humans have inhabited the earth, can we truly distinguish between the human and natural world? To what degree can wilderness really be preserved or restored once it has been degraded?

Then there is the underlying question of how we define wildness. Is it based on what the landscape looked like when conquering Europeans arrived? Is the glorification of wilderness the luxury of elite city dwellers who look down on rural culture?

These are theoretical questions, but the answers form the foundation for a concrete scientific approach. This study acknowledges the challenges and contradictions involved. While it does not claim to satisfy them, it offers several justifications for focusing on wildness.

First, the wildness approach doesn't demand purity. A spectrum of wildness may be recognized and valued, with smaller degrees still worth conserving.

The spotlight on wildness has other practical advantages. A single person can complete this kind of analysis in a reasonable time. It relies on evaluating the human footprint, which is not difficult to measure.

Creating the Wildness Model

The US Geological Survey's Gap Analysis Program is one of the nation's best known, most developed tools for conservation planning. It tracks biodiversity patterns in the landscape and covers most of the United States.

The Gap Analysis has three major objectives: 1) to produce accurate maps of land cover, 2) to create models that can predict where animal populations will live, and 3) to identify species whose habitat needs more conservation.

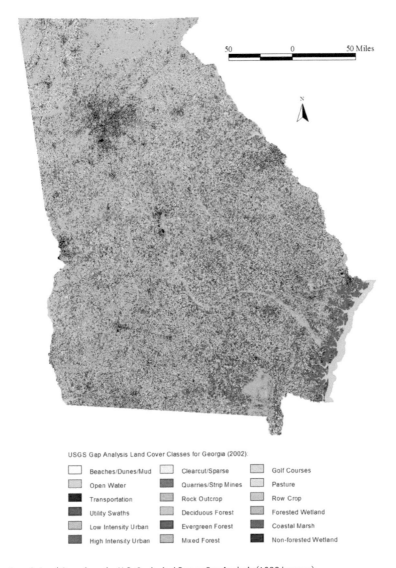

USGS Gap Analysis Land Cover Classes for Georgia (2002):

Beaches/Dunes/Mud	Clearcut/Sparse	Golf Courses
Open Water	Quarries/Strip Mines	Pasture
Transportation	Rock Outcrop	Row Crop
Utility Swaths	Deciduous Forest	Forested Wetland
Low Intensity Urban	Evergreen Forest	Coastal Marsh
High Intensity Urban	Mixed Forest	Non-forested Wetland

Georgia Land Cover from the U.S. Geological Survey Gap Analysis (1998 Imagery).

Watson's wildness model complements the Gap Analysis. The principle behind the wildness approach is to track how people have changed the landscape. Places with the least human impact, or footprint, have the greatest relative wildness. This isn't just about where people live, but where they created infrastructure to support their society: roads, railroads, the electric grid, nighttime lights, dams, etc.

Geographic information system (GIS) technology and remote sensing have enabled wildness mapping at the global, national, and sometimes regional level. But there have been few state-level assessments of landscape wildness.

The UGA analysis examined these categories to calculate wildness:

1. Human population density
2. Road density
3. Dominant type of land cover (i.e., forested wetland, low-intensity urban, pasture, etc.)
4. Distance from publicly managed land and/or land managed for conservation
5. Distance from known pollution sources
6. Distance from core black bear habitat

Each set of information was overlapped on a map. The map layers work like filters that, when combined, provide a balanced assessment of wildness.

The information fed into the model came from many sources, including the US Census Bureau, the Georgia Department of Transportation, and the Georgia Department of Natural Resources. Tracts of land were assigned different values for each of the six categories. This was often based on how far they were from places that humans have changed either a lot (roads, pollution sources) or very little (bear habitat, federal park land).

In many respects, pollution information proved the toughest to objectively evaluate and represent, so it was weighted less in calculating the wildness score.

There were some generalizations in the model. For example, all conservation lands are not equal, because they vary in size and have different managers and purposes. A plot of private timberland conserved from development is not necessarily as wild as a federal wildlife refuge.

50   0   50 Miles

N

■ Land Cover Classes Comprising >= 25% of Core Black Bear Habitat

▨ Land Cover Classes Comprising 6 - 24% of Core Black Bear Habitat

□ Land Cover Classes Comprising <= 5% of Core Black Bear Habitat

NOTE: The land cover dataset is derived from the U.S.G.S. Gap Analysis for Georgia (2002).

Georgia land cover from the U.S. Geological Survey Gap Analysis reclassified to highlight potential bear habitat quality (1998 Imagery).

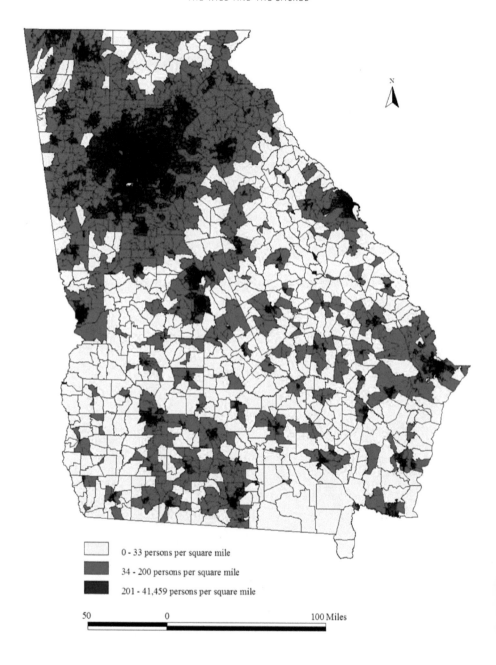

0 - 33 persons per square mile

34 - 200 persons per square mile

201 - 41,459 persons per square mile

| 50 | 0 | 100 Miles |

Poplulation density by Census 2000 block group.

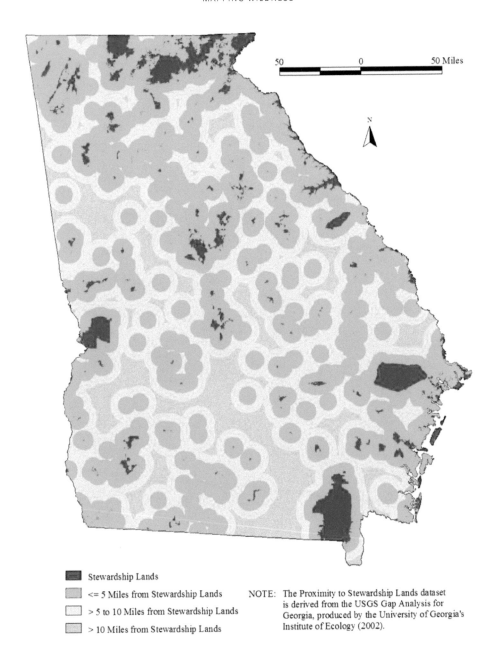

50   0   50 Miles

N

Stewardship Lands

<= 5 Miles from Stewardship Lands

> 5 to 10 Miles from Stewardship Lands

> 10 Miles from Stewardship Lands

NOTE: The Proximity to Stewardship Lands dataset is derived from the USGS Gap Analysis for Georgia, produced by the University of Georgia's Institute of Ecology (2002).

Proximity to stewardship lands as a variable in the determination of relative landscape wildness.

50   0   50 Miles

N

Road Density is derived from the
Georgia Department of Transportation
road network base map. (2002)

☐ 0 - 2.01 Miles Per Square Mile
▨ 2.02 - 15.05 Miles Per Square Mile
■ 15.06 - 37.99 Miles Per Square Mile

Road density as a variable in the determination of relative landscape wildderness.

Wildness Map: Key Findings

Few remaining areas outside Georgia's small wilderness network are likely to qualify under the strict legal definition of wilderness. However, the state still contains a surprising number of medium- to high-wildness areas. Some of these could be restored to greater wildness under public ownership or through conservation management.

The two wildest areas in the state, the Chattahoochee National Forest area in the north and the Okefenokee National Wildlife Refuge in the south, were already widely acknowledged as important wild spaces. However, the model revealed that the third-wildest area is a swath stretching along the Fall Line—the shore of a prehistoric sea—from southwest to north-central Georgia.

Most striking is the area south and east of Macon, between the Ocmulgee and Oconee rivers. This area is only about forty miles from two large federally managed public lands, the Piedmont National Wildlife Refuge and Oconee National Forest. Linking them with the Ocmulgee corridor wildlands would create an area comparable in size to the state's two premier wilderness areas.

The wildness model also identified the Altamaha River corridor in the southeastern part of the state as a significant wildland. It's worth noting that the Altamaha is fed by the Ocmulgee and Oconee. Linkages between the Altamaha and the nearby Okefenokee could provide movement corridors for bears and other wildlife between the state's southern and central wildlands. These potential links have since become a priority in the state's Wildlife Action Plan.

Integrating Biodiversity

The next question was how the areas revealed by this wildness model overlap with those emerging from available biodiversity models. The best comparison is with the Georgia Natural Heritage Program.

The Georgia Natural Heritage Program database catalogs places where rare and threatened species live. It was created in 1986 as a collaboration between the Nature Conservancy and the Georgia Department of Natural Resources, and is now a privately funded

A little blue heron at Ocmulgee. *Photo by Sharman Ayoub.*

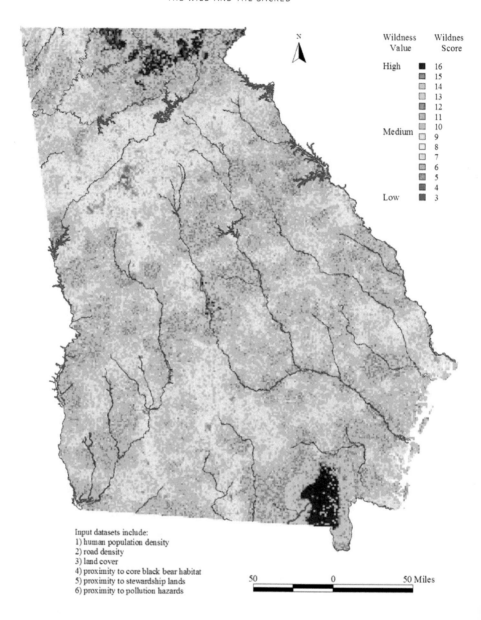

Input datasets include:
1) human population density
2) road density
3) land cover
4) proximity to core black bear habitat
5) proximity to stewardship lands
6) proximity to pollution hazards

Relative wildness of the Georgia landscape.

project of the Georgia Wildlife Resources Division's wildlife conservation section. The database is a comprehensive, well-organized system of records. But a decade ago when this research was done, the database had some significant limitations: the information came from a variety of sources that weren't equal in quality and detail, and the entries weren't dated. There was no way to distinguish between recent species sightings and records that were more historical in nature. Even so, the database is probably the best information set of its kind for Georgia.

The database was acquired for this study, reformatted, and mapped to display the occurrence of 1) animal species, 2) aquatic species, 3) plant species, and 4) all records combined. Rare species were given extra weight. The maps on the following pages illustrate these findings.

The records were used to create four different "heat" maps of species diversity. In some cases, the results were predictable; for example, high levels of animal and aquatic diversity occurred around rivers, especially the Flint and Altamaha. Rare plants seemed to be more spread across the state than animal and waterborne species, although many of the hot spots were similar.

A major conclusion of this analysis is that Georgia's river corridors are fundamentally important for biodiversity.

Although federal public lands are protected from major development, the analysis found they were less biodiverse than might be expected. While the Fort Stewart Army installation and the Chattahoochee National Forest had a rich array of special species, the Okefenokee didn't, at least according to the Natural Heritage Program database.

Swift Creek, a tributary of the Ocmulgee River. *Photo by Sharman Ayoub.*

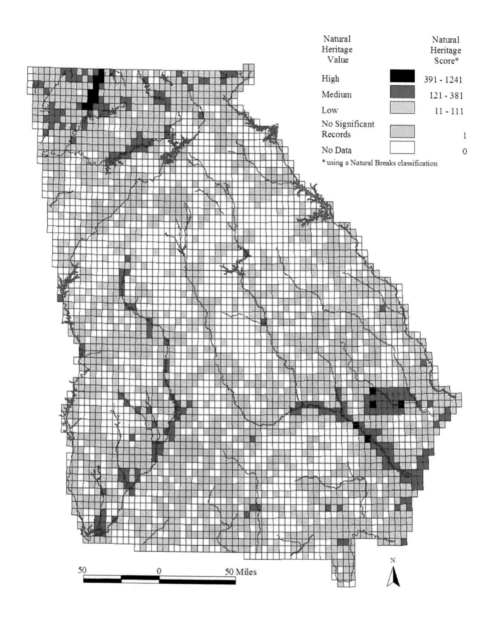

Distribution of weighted animal species element occurrences in the Georgia natural Heritage Program database (2002).

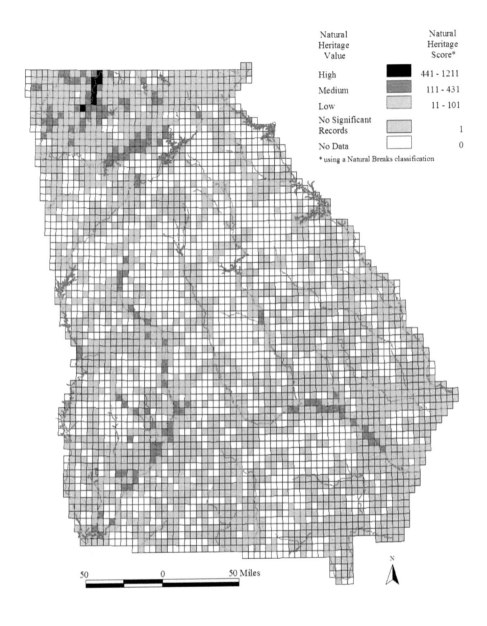

Distribution of weighted aquatic species element occurrences in the Georgia natural Heritage Program database (2002).

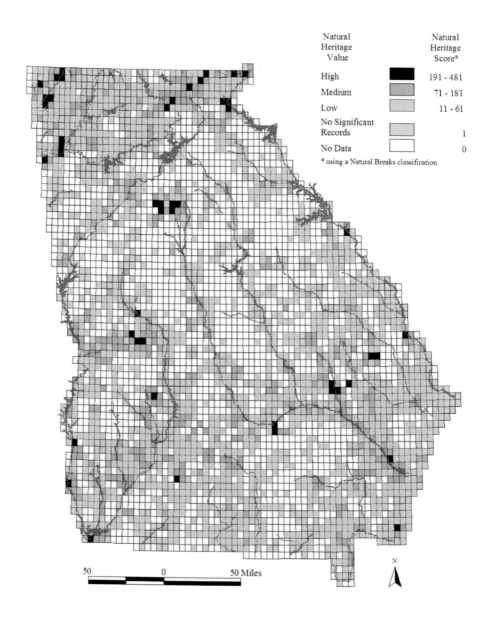

Distribution of weighted plant species element occurrences in the Georgia natural Heritage Program database (2002).

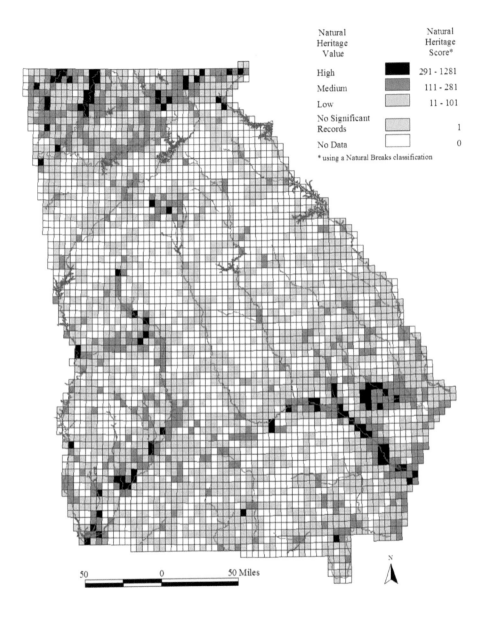

Natural Heritage Value | Natural Heritage Score*
High — 291 - 1281
Medium — 111 - 281
Low — 11 - 101
No Significant Records — 1
No Data — 0
* using a Natural Breaks classification

50   0   50 Miles

N

Distribution of weighted element occurrences for All species in the Georgia natural Heritage Program database (2002).

Neither did Middle Georgia's Oconee National Forest or the Piedmont and Bond Swamp national wildlife refuges, even though they have high wilderness value.

However, unlike the Okefenokee and Chattahoochee, Middle Georgia's large federal holdings were established in the second half of the twentieth century, on land that had been degraded by years of cotton farming. It may not have had time to recover its true biodiversity value.

Another key reason for its apparent lack of diversity, which comes up repeatedly in this study, could simply be a lack of information. The area had been largely skipped during scientific surveys of plants and animals. As a result, the level of biodiversity may be better labeled as "unknown." The area without data included one of the most prominent regions illuminated by the wilderness map: the region southeast of Macon and south of the Oconee National Forest and Piedmont National Wildlife Refuge.

Since this study was completed, more species records have been added to the Natural Heritage Program database within the mid-state Ocmulgee River watershed. Many are the result of highly focused searches for certain unusual species, such as robust red-horse fish and Ocmulgee skullcap plants. While knowledge is growing, there is still less broad biotic information about this region than about others in Georgia.

It seems likely that a dual-conservation strategy that combines biodiversity research *with* landscape wildness would better target Georgia's most significant conservation areas.

Storks and egrets gather in the wetlands near the Ocmulgee River. *Photo by Sharman Ayoub.*

Black bear in Oaky Woods. *Photo by Scott McDonald, courtesy Georgia Department of Natural Resources.*

BLACK BEARS IN MIDDLE GEORGIA

The black bear is the only species that gets its own category in the UGA wildness model. It's not listed as threatened or endangered. Yet it was chosen over rarer species, such as the red-cockaded woodpecker. Why?

There are key reasons for choosing large mammalian omnivores like the black bear:

1. As large omnivorous mammals, they are functionally similar to people;
2. The size of the range needed and how intensely the bears use the space;
3. The conflict occurs between their needs and the way humans carve up the landscape;
4. Managing for healthy bear populations also creates good habitat for many less charismatic species; and
5. Simplicity. (In Georgia, black bears are the only large mammalian omnivores—besides people.)

The Georgia Department of Natural Resources estimates Middle Georgia's black bear population at around 300, the smallest in the state.

Unlike bears in the mountains and southern coastal plain, Middle Georgia bears mostly roam on private land. However, the heart of their range overlaps with Oaky Woods and Ocmulgee state wildlife management areas.

These properties lie across the Ocmulgee River from each other, south of Warner Robins. They are partially state-owned but have eroded in size over the past fifteen years.

According to the Georgia Department of Natural Resources, Oaky Woods Wildlife Management Area was 17,800 acres and is now 12,750 acres. (On a positive note for conservation, what remains is all owned by state or county governments rather than being leased from a private company). Ocmulgee WMA is less than half its previous size of 32,000 acres.

The central Georgia bear population needs about 200 bears to be secure. According to common guidelines, that population would need between 500,000 acres and 1 million acres of habitat. But they have nowhere near that much: Middle Georgia's bears live on about 290,000 acres.

This study incorporates the idea that permanently conserving more bear habitat would help protect the state's largest remaining wild landscape and its wildlife.

Bear habitat conservation could be achieved in several ways. One is expanding the use of conservation easements on private forests and working lands. These easements are voluntary limits a landowner places on how the land can be used in the future in exchange for tax benefits. Another method is for the government to buy more land to preserve. A final possibility is a strategic combination of the two.

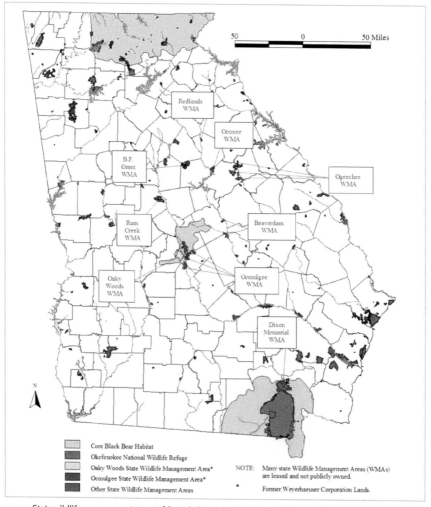

State wildlife management areas of Georgia in relation to core black bear habitats.

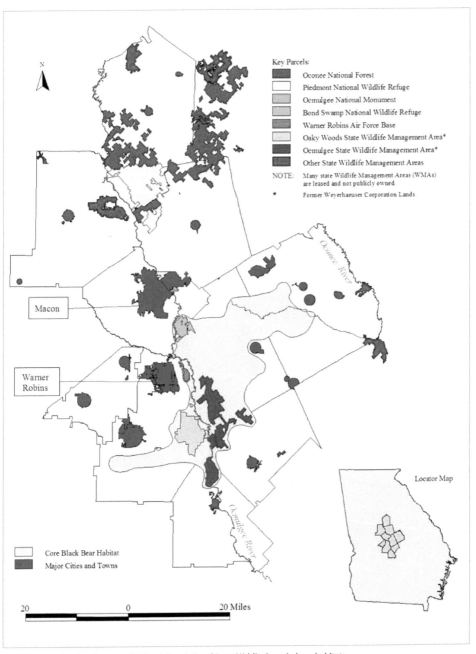

Key Parcels:

- Oconee National Forest
- Piedmont National Wildlife Refuge
- Ocmulgee National Monument
- Bond Swamp National Wildlife Refuge
- Warner Robins Air Force Base
- Oaky Woods State Wildlife Management Area*
- Ocmulgee State Wildlife Management Area*
- Other State Wildlife Management Areas

NOTE: Many state Wildlife Management Areas (WMAs) are leased and not publicly owned.

* Former Weyerhaeuser Corporation Lands

Macon

Warner Robins

Oconee River

Ocmulgee River

Locator Map

- Core Black Bear Habitat
- Major Cities and Towns

20   0   20 Miles

Federal and state public lands in relationship to Middle Georgia bear habitats.

The annual Ocmulgee Indigenous Celebration at Ocmulgee Mounds park draws members of tribes from across the country. *Photo by Sharman Ayoub.*

CHAPTER 4

The Muscogee in Georgia

Rebuilding Ties

Although the Muscogee (Creek) people were driven west by the United States government in the early 1800s, the Muscogee Creek Nation began to reassert a broader interest in Georgia in the early 1990s. Its involvement was sparked by a road project that could have irreparably harmed sites held sacred by the tribe.

First, it should be noted that all Muscogee do not have a single government and identity, any more than all Indigenous or all Americans do.

Headquartered in Okmulgee Oklahoma, the Muscogee (Creek) Nation is the fourth largest federally recognized tribe in the United States with more than 89,000 citizens. But there are many other independent Muscogee tribes and tribal towns. Tribes include the Alabama-Coushatta Tribe of Texas, the Coushatta Tribe of Louisiana, and the Poarch Band in Alabama. Tribal towns include Kialegee, Thlopthlocco, and Alabama-Quassarte towns in Oklahoma.

Southeastern Native Americans have a relationship with the Ocmulgee region spanning about 17,000 years, to when the first Paleo Indians arrived in what is now Georgia. Their descendants eventually began farming and trading with other regions. That earlier society's power and complexity peaked between A.D. 1,000 and 1,500. This "Mississippian period" is when most scholars believe the monumental mounds were built at Ocmulgee, although some Muscogee place the date much earlier.

The moon rises over the Earth Lodge at Ocmulgee Mounds National Historical Park. *Photo by Sharman Ayoub.*

From the Mississippian culture, there eventually emerged the historic Muscogee (Creek) Confederacy, one of the strongest tribes in the Southeast at the time of European settlement. The settlers dubbed the tribe "the Creeks," reflecting their strong ties to the rivers and their tributaries.

A rapid series of treaties pushed these Native Americans west. By 1805, the Ocmulgee River was the dividing line between Indian Territory and the state of Georgia. The Muscogee retained only a three-by-five-mile strip of land east of the river known as the Old Ocmulgee Fields Reserve. The area was regarded as the cradle of the Muscogee Confederacy, an early union of tribal towns.

During the next few decades, the Creeks fought internally over how to deal with aggressive state and federal governments. All of the Muscogee were forced to surrender their lands by 1826, when a (disputed) treaty abolished all Creek holdings in Georgia. Most Muscogee emigrated to Oklahoma, while others dispersed into Alabama and Florida.

For generations after Indian removal, the scattered Muscogee were able to maintain few ties to Georgia, although some made personal pilgrimages.

Among Muscogee groups, the Muscogee Creek Nation may be the most active in asserting its right to a voice in decisions about the tribe's traditional heritage sites in the Southeast. Federal laws now require that tribes be consulted on certain types of development or infrastructure projects.

Indians from many tribes share traditional folkways at the annual Ocmulgee Indigenous Celebration at Ocmulgee Mounds National Historical Park. *Photo by Sharman Ayoub.*

Sacred Space: The Traditional Cultural Property

When the concept for the Ocmulgee National Monument was originally approved in 1934, it was envisioned to include 2,000 acres commonly known as the Ocmulgee Old Fields, named for the land that had once been reserved by the Muscogee. That vision was scaled back to fewer than 700 acres—a small fraction of "the Old Ocmulgee Fields"—because funding was so scarce during the Depression. It included the forty-five-acre Lamar Mounds, featuring the only intact spiral mound in North America. But the Lamar section was (and currently is) separated from the main body of the park by private land.

A highway project first drew attention to the biggest problem with the scaled-down version of the park, which separated the monument from the Lamar Mounds with private land.

The Georgia Department of Transportation proposed an extension of the Eisenhower Parkway, a section of US Highway 90. To relieve congestion on this route between Columbus and Savannah, the Macon section of this "Fall Line Freeway" would be realigned across the wetlands dividing the Ocmulgee Mounds

Left, Sylvia Flowers, who was a ranger at Ocmulgee National Monument, led Muscogee (Creek) representatives on a hike to the Lamar mound complex after flooding in the early 1990s. Right, native activists visited the Ocmulgee National Monument during the early 1990s to fight the planned route of the Eisenhower Expressway through the Old Fields. This man was part of the Trail of Tears Motorcycle Ride, which carried this flag to Chattanooga before continuing to Okmulgee, OK, capital of the Muscogee (Creek) Nation. *Photos courtesy of Sylvia Flowers.*

A representative from the Georgia DOT, park ranger Sylvia Flowers, Muscogee Creek Nation historic preservation officer/consultant Alan Cook, local environmentalist John Wilson, and Don Barger of the National Parks Conservation Association discuss the Fall Line Freeway project. *Photo courtesy of Sylvia Flowers.*

from the isolated Lamar section. The route, proposed in the 1990s, was opposed by both the Muscogee Creek Nation and the National Park Service.

Under US Indian law, the American government must consult with tribes before using federal dollars on projects that might affect tribal rights. The Georgia Department of Transportation originally argued that this rule didn't apply because the route was on private land. But GDOT eventually came to recognize the region's true significance to the Muscogee and the federal legal obligations to consider tribal opinion.

Laws Governing Native American Cultural Resources

National Historic Preservation Act (1966): Created National Register of Historic Places and provided framework for Traditional Cultural Properties.

National Transportation Act (1966): Required cultural resources to be considered/avoided in transportation projects, and required that tribes be consulted.

The National Environmental Policy Act (1969): Required cultural resources to be considered/avoided in federally funded projects, and required that tribes be consulted.

American Indian Religious Freedom Act (1978): Granted Native Americans access to traditional places on federal lands for religious observances, and allowed the right to collect and use sacred items such as eagle feathers.

Native American Graves Protection and Repatriation Act (1990): Mandated the return to the tribes of "human remains, funerary objects, sacred objects, and objects of cultural patrimony" that were held by federal agencies, museums, and other institutions.

In response, the tribe pursued designating a large part of the landscape as a Traditional Cultural Property (TCP). A Traditional Cultural Property is a listing on the National Register of Historic Places that recognizes an area's association with the beliefs and cultural practices of a living community. These beliefs and practices are rooted in its history and important to its identity. At the time, there were no Traditional Cultural Properties recognized east of the Mississippi River.

The Muscogee drew a suggested boundary based on the "Old Fields Reserve" of the 1805 treaty. The Keeper of the National Register approved the Old Fields Traditional Cultural Property in 1999 but shrank the boundary to exclude previous development.

Even so, the designation solidified the Muscogee right to be consulted on decisions about the Eisenhower Extension as well as future projects within the boundary.

Eventually, local support shifted in favor of Ocmulgee Mounds park expansion rather than building a (very expensive) highway through the swamp. The Eisenhower Extension project died a slow death over the following decade.

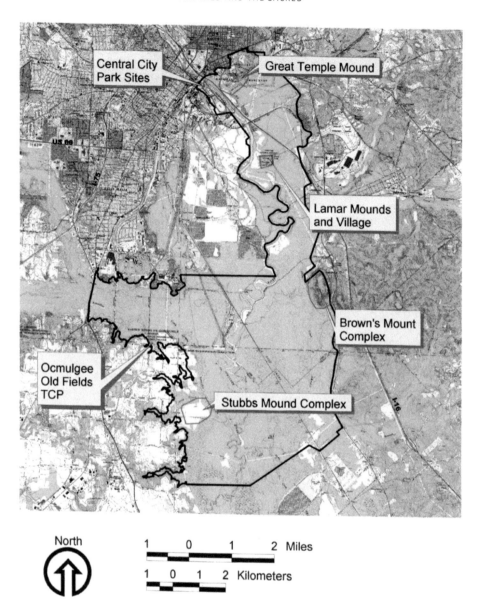

North

1   0   1   2 Miles

1   0   1   2 Kilometers

Ocmulgee Old Fields Traditional Cultural Property (1999). *Courtesy of Sylvia Flowers, National Park Service (2007).*

Issues Raised by the Culture Gap

The road project highlighted some of the fundamental differences between the worldviews of the Muscogee and current residents of their former homeland.

The UGA study sought to use a detailed survey to learn Muscogee ideas, priorities, and visions for the Middle Georgia landscape.

A list of potential Muscogee contacts in Oklahoma was developed in consultation with John Wilson, Sylvia Flowers (a retired master ranger with the National Park Service), and Alan Cook (a Muscogee historic preservation consultant). Recipients were recommended because of their service in Muscogee government or cultural preservation.

Only five people completed the 2007 survey, but their responses provided a glimpse into the Muscogee perspective on land ownership, cultural resources, and partnerships.

Mainstream American society tends to regard human culture as something that happens outside nature. But the Muscogee idea of "cultural resources" includes the

Members of the Muscogee (Creek) Nation Royalty and the Muscogee Nation Honor Guard attend the Ocmulgee Indgenous Celebration. *Photo by Sharman Ayoub.*

landscape itself. The idea encompasses not only plants and animals, but all components of natural surroundings: water, weather, the horizon, and the view of the sun and the stars. Giving a Traditional Cultural Property boundaries on a map separates its physical and spiritual aspects.

To many Natives, even using the word "property" for a place with spiritual meaning is offensive (and a drawback to the "Traditional Cultural Property" concept). The term "cultural resource" implies that cultural sites are commodities to be used and bartered.

One survey participant argued that the full cultural context of a Native site can only be understood if it remains undisturbed. An example is the discovery that mounds in Arkansas align with

Toddlers from different cultures meet at the Ocmulgee Indigenous Celebration at Ocmulgee Mounds National Historical Park. *Photo by Sharman Ayoub.*

astronomical events. If some mounds in this location had been destroyed, or if the horizon had been blocked, their significance as an engineering feat would have been lost.

The Muscogee Creek worldview provides a framework for the tribe's approach to its ancestral lands in Georgia. But one respondent pointed out that the Muscogee Creek Nation's policy is as likely to be driven by economic needs in Oklahoma, as by preservation concerns in the historic homeland in Georgia.

One person expressed a concern that economic benefits to the tribe could trump cultural preservation. In other words, it's not enough to protect cultural sites from non-Muscogee development. Muscogee society needs to make a commitment that it will not exploit them either.

All of the Muscogee survey participants supported expanding Ocmulgee Mounds into a national park. However, some also emphasized the importance of the tribe playing an active role in defining and interpreting its own culture.

Features Associated with Traditional Muscogee Practices

Muscogee traditional cultural practices and spiritual beliefs are often associated with certain kinds of artifacts or features. Many of them are associated with the Traditional Cultural Property in and around the Ocmulgee Mounds.

They include:

1. mound sites,

2. ceremonial earth lodges,

3. square grounds (usually with a sacred fire at the center of a ceremonial plaza),

4. stylized hawk designs,

5. old fields representing abandoned farm fields,

6. stone rings,

7. medicine rocks, and

8. places with traditionally important plant resources (such as groves).

Deer crossing in front of the Earth Lodge on a misty morning. *Photo by Sharman Ayoub.*

Geese take off from a winter stop at Ocmulgee Mounds National Historical Park. *Photo by Sharman Ayoub.*

CHAPTER 5

Following
the River's Trail

The UGA study results were used to develop concrete suggestions for policymakers who want to protect Georgia's remaining wild lands. Although the research was originally requested by the Wilderness Society, the National Parks Conservation Association (another nonprofit, where Watson now works) has been the advocacy group primarily influenced by it. While many of the recommendations weren't followed explicitly, they guided a strategy that has already led to the initial expansion of the Ocmulgee Mounds park. Some of Watson's recommendations may be out of date, but most remain relevant. It's not too late to take many of these steps.

Recommendations addressed three primary themes:
1. the implications of the wildness model and ways to expand it;
2. advancing the national park and preserve idea, or some similar concept; and
3. increasing Muscogee involvement in Georgia conservation efforts, especially in identifying Native cultural sites for protection.

Expanding on the
Landscape Wilderness Model

First, Watson suggested that the landscape wildness model could be expanded to support a Southeastern conservation program spanning the Piedmont in Georgia, Alabama, and South Carolina. Often associated with red clay soils, the Piedmont is the

geologic plateau between the coastal plain and the Appalachian foothills.

This kind of regional outlook could be especially attractive to potential land trust partners such as the Georgia-Alabama Land Trust and the Nature Conservancy. Other interested groups also operate or cooperate across the region. For example, the Georgia Wildlife Federation has sister organizations in Alabama and South Carolina. The Muscogee Creek Nation is interested in protecting cultural sites throughout their historic homelands in the southeast.

Since this research was conducted, progress has been made on collecting and analyzing more regional science data through the South Atlantic Landscape Conservation Cooperative and the Southeast Conservation Adaptation Strategy. By synthesizing their accomplishments with other research, Watson's model could be extended not only geographically, but by incorporating more kinds of information. For example, the UGA model's depiction of pollution impacts could be made more precise.

Watson recommended that archaeological data also be added to the landscape maps using a state database that catalogs ancient and historic sites. In 2018, Mercer University followed this recommendation, publishing a study that analyzed existing Ocmulgee corridor archaeological records. Integrating this information into a wildlands assessment could be a bridge between the interests of nature lovers and cultural preservationists.

Further strides could be made in developing and carrying out regional policy based on all this new research.

Watson praised the original Wilderness Society concept of developing a collaboration between private landowners and conservationists. The idea was for landowners to voluntarily register their property as part of a state or regional conservation network.

This recommendation has since come to pass in the form of the National Conservation Easement Database, a public-private partnership made up of local and regional land trusts, national conservation groups, and local, state, and federal agencies.

Pursuing a Bigger Park

Partnerships will also be key to creating a larger park and preserve along the Ocmulgee River.

Since this study, two key organizations were founded or expanded to support this effort: the Ocmulgee National Park & Preserve Initiative and the Ocmulgee Land Trust. These active, local organizations have had a big impact on building public and political support for conservation and park expansion.

Around the time Congress approved the 2019 Ocmulgee Mounds park boundary expansion, additional conservation nonprofits also became more active players. Among them are the Georgia Conservancy, the Open Space Institute, and The Nature Conservancy.

Others, such as the Trust for Public Land and the Archaeological Conservancy, are also potential partners. The Archaeological Conservancy is the only national organization specializing in acquiring significant archaeological sites. The conservancy has

Lantern light tours are held each year at Ocmulgee Mounds National Historical Park during Macon's Cherry Blossom Festival. *Photo by Sharman Ayoub.*

Visitors to Ocmulgee Mounds watch a king snake unwind. *Photos by Sharman Ayoub.*

been holding about 300 acres for the Ocmulgee Mounds park since they were first donated by the McCall family decades ago. The conservancy is now in the process of transferring that property to the national historical park.

Watson recommended that a stakeholder group be created to contribute to an informal special-resource study. It would use National Park Service criteria to guide research supporting the case for a larger Ocmulgee park and preserve.

Since Watson's recommendation was made, the Park Service has started some of this work itself. It completed a smaller-scale boundary expansion study and is in the midst of an official special-resource study.

But researchers—particularly at Mercer University—have informally jump-started this process by compiling information about the region's archaeology, birds, and rare plants. Their work is framing the issue and providing information for the Park Service to consider, as suggested.

Watson emphasizes that hunters should be included in any stakeholder group shaping the park and preserve concept. Hunters have been some of the most vocal in expressing concerns about a strict national park idea. They have voiced the belief that state managers are more sympathetic to hunting than the federal government would be.

Photo by Sharman Ayoub.

However, the main goal among park proponents is a national park *and preserve*—with the preserve portions reserved for hunting. Hunters could help design the size of the preserve so it not only protects, but expands, public hunting. The national park component could be limited to archaeological and cultural sites.

The UGA study noted that park advocates could bolster hunting rights on a much grander scale by pushing to extend the preserve further downstream, along most of the Ocmulgee and Altamaha rivers. A 2004 resolution by both chambers of the Georgia General Assembly supported this idea. That region is already home to six additional wildlife management areas.

Hearing Muscogee Voices

The UGA study demonstrated the overlapping benefits of protecting the natural ecosystems of the Ocmulgee corridor and the ancestral lands of the Muscogee Indians.

The importance of the Muscogee Creek Nation's success in creating the Ocmulgee Old Fields Traditional Cultural Property has never been fully recognized. But it paved the way for a larger Muscogee presence in the Macon area.

Even a decade ago, the UGA study identified property ownership as a key to establishing the Muscogee Nation as an active decision-maker in Georgia. Although the tribe's historic and spiritual connection to the land is well established, history has proven that property ownership is the way Euro-Americans control land use.

Since 2019, the Muscogee Creek Nation can now claim that stake: it bought 121 acres on top of Brown's Mount in November of that year. The land includes important parts of the ancient archaeological site that weren't on state property. The Ocmulgee Land Trust and the Ocmulgee National Park & Preserve Initiative helped facilitate the purchase.

The property may present a chance for the tribe to eventually acquire the state-owned part of Brown's Mount. Watson suggested that this might be an opportunity for the Muscogee to establish a tribal historical park there, possibly in partnership with the National Park Service. (There is even an "NPS-Affiliated Area" designation available for such situations.)

The UGA study urges Georgia conservationists to actively seek Muscogee participation and viewpoints. Members of the tribe should be involved in land preservation planning and decision-making.

The Muscogee Creek Nation should also be in charge of the public interpretation of their history and culture. Native tribes already play a vital role in the largest event at the Ocmulgee Mounds National Historical Park: the annual Indigenous celebration. Because the Ocmulgee mounds are considered an important cultural site by many tribes—not just the Muscogee—Native representatives, dancers, and reenactors come from across the country each year for a weekend of living history, crafts, and dancing that draws about 15,000 visitors. The park forged closer ties with these tribes over the years by collaborating with them on planning.

The Muscogee could similarly help develop programs for Fort Hawkins, the site of an early frontier trading post and American

Left, native teenagers visit in traditional warrior regalia at the Ocmulgee Indigenous Celebration. Right, native performers from across the U.S. demonstrate traditional dances, such as this hoop dance, at the annual Ocmulgee Indigenous Celebration. *Photos by Sharman Ayoub.*

military encampment, now owned by the City of Macon. The tribe could help accurately depict its ancestors' roles at this former border crossing, which is currently open only certain days with limited programming.

A Muscogee living-history village located somewhere between Macon and Hawkinsville could give the Nation a chance to tell its own story, either as part of a larger Ocmulgee Park and Preserve, or in partnership with it. Such an attraction could even become a center for cross-cultural education and research, similar to Colonial Williamsburg in Virginia. Williamsburg operates a foundation and a teacher-training institute; publishes journals, books, and multimedia educational materials; and sponsors historical and archaeological research, workshops, and conferences.

The Muscogee could re-create a traditional village, with re-enactors depicting Native residents of the time. Here, a re-enactor at Ocmulgee Mounds portrays naturalist William Bartram, who traveled through Georgia cataloguing plants and attended some of the Creek treaty negotiations before U.S. Independence. *Photo by Sharman Ayoub.*

A similar Muscogee historical site could help rebuild the connection between the tribe and its historic homeland while passing to a younger generation traditional skills, crafts, botanical lore, and construction methods.

Tribal ownership of more land in Middle Georgia might further benefit both the Muscogee economy and the environment.

A highlight of the annual Ocmulgee Indigenous Celebration at the Ocmulgee Mounds is when visitors are invited to join Indian dancers. *Photo by Sharman Ayoub.*

For example, a sustainable timber industry, owned and operated by the Muscogee, could be established in collaboration with conservationists and the state land trust community. Such a project could also foster spin-off endeavors for the tribe in woodcrafts, furniture making, and carbon credit trading.

Other Recommendations

The study concludes with several other recommendations for conservationists. These include a greater focus on the Middle Georgia black bear population and increased state ownership of Wildlife Management Areas.

The report notes that black bear conservation hasn't received enough attention in Georgia, particularly for the mid-state bears whose habitat is mostly on private land. Local celebrations, such as a Black Bear or Frontier Days festival, similar to those developed by towns in other states, could build public support for protecting black bear habitat or for highlighting an important chapter of the region's history.

Landscape modeling has progressed since this study was first published, leading to several Georgia priority plans that make

Photo by Scott McDonald, courtesy the Georgia Department of Natural Resources.

the Ocmulgee corridor a conservation priority. The Strategic Bear Management Plan, the Georgia State Wildlife Action Plan, and the State Forest Action Plan have all been developed to provide tools for making better policy decisions. Unfortunately, these tools aren't often used by other agencies responsible for permitting and compliance. As a result, clear-cutting has increased noticeably, and a large-scale solar development was allowed to be sited in a portion of core bear habitat near the river. So far, the state priority plans have done little to guide these kinds of activities to more appropriate locations. All state agencies should be using these plans to inform their decisions.

Middle Georgia's black bears depend heavily on the habitat preserved in Oaky Woods and Ocmulgee wildlife management areas. Watson recommended increasing state ownership of more acreage within the wildlife management area system. At the time of the study, Georgia had a large system of these, but less than half were state-owned. The rest were leased. That meant the state could give up leases to save money during an economic down-turn or owners could end the leases and choose to use the land differently. This uncertainty makes for an unstable system for conserving wildlife resources over the long haul.

But the rate of state ownership has improved already. Today, sixty-four of the state's 111 wildlife management areas are majori-ty-owned by the state. (Many include a combination of owned and leased land.) All but eight of the remaining wildlife management areas are leased primarily from another branch of government or an educational institution.

The new Georgia Outdoor Stewardship Trust Fund, which was approved by voters through a referendum, began providing grants in 2019 to support parks and trails and buy land. These purchases are intended to target property critical to wildlife, clean water, and outdoor recreation. The fund could help with additional WMA land purchases.

Mapping the Future

The landscape model developed as part of this UGA study proved an effective way to identify critical areas for conservation. The process revealed that a large swath of Middle Georgia maintains significant wildness. Both the landscape and biodiversity models showed the importance of rivers as havens of diversity and connectors of isolated wild land.

Unfortunately, it's unclear how much of the land identified remains wild a decade later. Nevertheless, the current Department of the Interior study of the Ocmulgee corridor presents a unique opportunity to examine the concept of creating a park and preserve or something like it. It has the potential to encompass a swath of landscape that is rich in history and wildlife. However, the opportunity will pass unless lovers of the outdoors from all backgrounds find common ground to support the effort. Following more of these recommendations could provide tremendous long-term benefits to Middle Georgians, Muscogee people, and the wildlife with which they share a home.

A long exposure captures the trails of light created by visitors holding lanterns as they wend their way among the Ocmulgee mounds. *Photo by Sharman Ayoub.*

Photo by Sharman Ayoub.